SPORE

OR

SEED

Caitlin Maling is from Western Australia. She holds a doctorate in literature from the University of Sydney, an MFA in poetry from the University of Houston and is a previous recipient of the Marten Bequest in Poetry, the Val Vallis Award, and the John Marsden Poetry Prize. Previous collections from Caitlin Maling are *Conversations I've Never Had*, which was shortlisted for the Mary Gilmore Award and the Western Australian Premier's Book Awards, *Border Crossing*, *Fish Song* and *Fish Work*, which was highly commended in the 2020 Dorothy Hewett Award. *Spore or Seed* is her fifth book of poetry.

www.caitlinmaling.com

SPORE OR SEED

Caitlin Maling

To CGMH

Contents

spore or seed 9

One: Weeks 11

A Measured Risk 13
The Garden 14
In Bed 15
You are currently transformed 17
Succour 18
Navel Gazing 20
Little Oracle 21
Online Guided Meditation 22
38.6 / 39 23
39.6 24

Two: In Process 25

Three: Crowning 31

Four: It Is Hard to Become Accustomed to Being Food 39

Let Down 41
I Write Poems When I Wake at 1.30am to Pump 42
The breast not fed on for 36 hours 43
A Fairytale 44
In the part of the brain that regulates time 45
Withdrawal 46
If we ever imagined 47
Winter 49
What begins (four weeks) 50
The Nothing 51
It's Cold Inside the Café 52
I No Longer Feel the Throb 53
Your feet rise like teeth in the open 54

Five: The Death Section 55

The Following Is True 57
39.0 58
Your son died 59
Woo 60
The End Results of Need 61
Poem to My Aunt 62
2020 64
I Am Made Fuzzy by Grief 65
Covered in Crumbs and Contagion 66
A House Big Enough to Never Leave 67
First Holiday 68
Love 69

Six: #2020 71

Self-plagiarism: Ode to WillyWeather 73
Escape 74
You have to 75
Not Imagining Elsewhere 77
Of Human Bondage 78
I love the way that Ammons 79
Bathers Beach 80
Cruel 81
The truth about the end of the world 82
Day Care Day 83
Every Day I Call the Honeyeater by the Wrong Name 85
I want to write a joyful poem 86

Seven: These Poems Are Mostly Private Letters, Poems after Randolph Stow 87

Calliope 89
Dear Son / A Wind From the Sea 91
Child Portraits with Background 92
Landscapes 93
Sea Children, See Children 94

Eight: Even Unfit Mothers Have Fit Arms 95

Uniform 97
My Whole Life 100
I Do Not Feel Beheaded 101
Your Taste in People Will Change When You Learn to Love Yourself 102
Don't All Mothers Wish Immortality 103
The Sermon on the Mount 104
Brothers, Leeches and Being Turnt Inside Out 105
In Writing About Cain 108
Sometimes if I read a very good poem 109
Don't Doubt 110
I eat my grapefruit 112
Six Months 114

Nine: From Tumbleweed to Tick 115

Acknowledgements and works cited 126

spore or seed

you do not hum
or desire, you do
not thirst, hunger
or long, you linger
indivisible from dust
the smallest shadow
of the same sun
the days don't end
but begin and re-begin
this is not a reboot
of your father's favourite
TV show, but a season
a migration, nesting
spawning is this
what you need and this
who makes it through
the net? what pollen and manna
such timid ecstasy, the tongue
then the colour, the ending
then a blending

One: Weeks

A Measured Risk

Our home is safe,
our yard without any large trees
for you to jump from.
Your father has kind hands
and a low voice
he only raises to tell the dog
'don't'. I have only once
threatened murder – your aunt
barely older than you
in the kitchen. We shall not
have a second child.
There are corners though
and dark places.
Where you are now
has no edge
and is lit like amber.
The world is no jewel.
Lichen grows
on the roof tiles
and I pay a man
to kill the bugs
in the carpet. One day
my father left me.
I cannot say
yours will not
do the same.

The Garden

Your father discusses where to put the plants
        whether to pull up bricks
to get to irrigation.

We are new to dirt
        to digging, my hands
the type to need, not to knead.

The garden grows ugly
        at winter, hedges yellowing
the ends of things in pots shrivelling.

I'm slowly reintroducing activity
        to my day like coming off a diet
and the movement of fronds in wind

is suspicious. On Wednesday
        I watch you appear dirty and grainy
moving outside of colour.

Your arms and legs without a breeze
        show me how easy it is
to grow or let go.

In Bed

I tell my husband
foetuses open their eyes
from about eight weeks
but can only see from twenty

A friend of mine
also expecting
has paid for extra scans
to prove the baby
does indeed
lurk within her

We all have
different standards
of proof I cannot
put it plainer
than that

I am not colour-blind
but often forget
the right word
for what colour

Inside the womb
I imagine
is only red and black

Except it's never
not just that
but all the other
multisyllabic
pesky shades

Although, maybe
for the baby
the rods and cones
still in their hundreds
keep even
the ambiguity of clouds
and greys
at bay

You are currently transformed

with velum into your own
velvet box, pushing
like a seal against the red
weed of womb, I clasp
at any indication
of our sameness, ever the colour
of threads binding us
together. At night
in the twilight of your waking
and my own non-sleeping hours
your father lies against my side
and speaks so both of us hum
with his words, though only I
can feel you turning
resolutely solid
with your own gravity.

Succour

The fish fail.
The shellfish normally flown north
still reef-embedded.

I lie on my left side
like a mountain range
so the oxygen passes

unimpeded along the aorta.
In the garden
bees buzz

and sparrows squeak.
What happened
to all the less noble

characters of myth?
Did they persist
in shapeshifting?

Still move
across the boundaries
like prayers?

I grew
in a rickety home
with parched lawn

and trees to fall from
but am hidden now
by brown walls

and paved yard.
I shall never
touch skin

or peel
carapace from flesh
but I insist

on living
is that
the same?

Navel Gazing

My belly button pops out
like the tie at an end of a balloon.
I have dug into its recesses for years
thinking there might be a way to unspool it
peek inside or blow in another mouthful of air.
As I age, I like the idea of this gnarled thing
living at my centre like the nub
of a nut or the husked coconut.
Something secret even from me, and my prying
loose of all that's unfixed.
I have you to thank for this small notion
of something long kept hidden, a link
to being longed for while I press my hand
against the smooth unpliable skin of my stomach
and feel you press back.

Little Oracle

Each morning wakes me startled
your hiccups like satellites
blinking softly against the sky.

I have loved so little
and never for so faint a moment.
Every morning wakes me startled

the light reappearing behind the curtains
your father's footsteps, then shadow,
blinking softly against the sky.

He holds me, then puts his face to you.
Together we imagine you blinking
opening your eyes to the morning, startled

by colour, the feathering of eyelashes
against your cheeks, your own
blinking softly against the sky.

I am an orb and turn on an axis
that shifts as you sway,
each morning shakes me, startled
and blinking. Soft against the sky.

Online Guided Meditation

Where you rustle around
I picture a pig rifting
with snout for mushrooms. I do not
know when I will think of you
as anything other than animal.
I would not eat a pet, but would
the pig that is not mine, this sits
less easy with your trotters under my ribs.
'It's all a particular type of chaos then,' I say
to the bird in the bottlebrush. I leash
yours and call it mine.

38.6 / 39

warmth like extra light off the moon
weeks equivalent to a fever
rising / eventually they'll say
too far and pop the balloon
to let the heat out / day by day

i fight the restlessness
some birds fly / or swim
ten miles away and back
it can't just be for food

(at least in analogy)
like all fever visions
mine finds water
above and below

maybe this true jealousy
is of your immersion
warm as it may be
and my fear / to give you

only to a world
also broke open
by fever

39.6

I become as unwelcome as whale song
projected over a speaker late at night
at the caravan park Outback O'Bourke.

Sometimes I recognise the parents of famous people
at coffee stores, maybe it's a pandemic thing
or the unfamiliar familiar of impending motherhood.

I miss being loved in unbelievable ways.
I do not believe them, did not,
and was proved right in the end.

I have started to swell, like the gullet
of a humpback in the agony
of sifting plankton from water that should by all rights

be frozen. 'That's hysterical,
darling,' says the woman at the table next to me
before her elderly father arrives.

Someday I too will be out of my misery.
I crawl into my bundle of blankets to prepare for birth,
wondering if, to the whale, the water is soft.

Two: In Process

The question of form arises.

It is possible, I learn, to feel the tension of a curve, the sharp under the smooth.

The constant momentum of being a staging ground for growth.

//

I can never know where you are exactly, a murky constellation of might-be-limbs cushioned by fluid.

Sometimes there's a ripple, a quiver, or you press against the meniscus like I've caught a shadow, a fish on the line at the point where it starts to catch the surface light.

//

There's a field somewhere at the heart of this.

In birth visualisation exercises, I picture a moon gate arced, brick and overgrown with ivy. Light on the other side. I am always looking at it from afar. Sometimes a figure stands at centre, cowled and cowed.

The poetic field rarely has children in it, often gods, often desire.

//

I have to be willing to let the body be turned inside out.

I have to be a tunnel without sides, only round. A tunnel like through a piece of spaghetti, or down the barrel of a tank. I should not imagine tanks. A sometimes friend of mine has lost a childhood friend to a terrorist attack. This is a rupture, a rapture. He tries different ways to write it. Lately detective noir.

In the seminal LA noir *Chinatown*, they've stolen the water, a bomb is threatened, Faye Dunaway has had her dad's baby and somehow Jack Nicholson is attractive: rupture, rapture and a breaking of waters.

//

The great thesis that you cannot write after great loss, does it hold up under great individual joy that gets repeated so constantly as to become communal?

There is no one who can tell me this will not remake me.

//

I'm sure someone somewhere has described birth as an eruption.

//

Eighteen years old I am at Pompeii, below the now still singular shadow of Mt Vesuvius. The charred figures of villagers rest in catacombs, it's impossible to tell who has birthed and who might be cremated waiting for birth, if, at first, something of the pink of flesh held at core.

//

How can living plants manage both the masculine and the feminine? I'm hungry and this is the thought that comes first into the field.

We are all a list of thwarted longings.

//

I am sorry to bring you only offerings of terror, I try to write as I tread – softly – but the weight of you even forces my feet to sound where once they whispered, one of many foreshocks leading to your eruption.

//

My sometimes friend writes letters about fatherhood. They are beautiful. They have sentences in them as finely wrought as funeral urns or individual clay beads baked for prayer. I too would like to know which direction to face the divine and to kneel.

The problem with these letters is that they are trying to convince somebody of something, but I am unsure of the recipient and the message. They seem a suspicious way to waste beauty. I never doubt he loves his son.

If I were able to turn these letters upside down and shake them, nothing would fall out. You do have to admire a weave that holds like that.

//

To return to the question of form, I have never wanted to be obliterated, which is less obvious than it seems.

Another man I know, in the process of giving up alcohol, also gave up orgasm. Both, he said, ran the risk of shattering you. There was queer theory in his reasoning and also an illustration of Saints in exile dying from arrows piercing the body. Ecstasy, he said.

I think it's Apocrypha that some women orgasm as the crown of the head shatters through the cervix.

//

This is what I almost write to the sometimes friend:

I cannot mother because I have never reckoned with desire.

In one letter he says he sometimes forgets in the interstices of days to let them want you.

'To want you' is on a separate line.

//

A volcano cannot want, but a bomb is nothing but desire being rendered on other bodies. It seems likely I read this somewhere.

My work is nothing of the body and the work of mothering is only body, one a volcano, the other a bomb.

I think about writing a letter to the sometimes friend, but if I write the letter I will never write the poem.

//

I would offer a list:

I am the gristle that's grown up around the wound. I will regret the evidence of my body not having been so solely mine. Every point of mine left angular hurts, even when pressed again softness. But this is a wound of the flesh: bloody and multiplying.

I clutch at bones, grow the scar tissue.

A war to remain.

Three: Crowning

i.
This is not the beginning
but the view from the window:
a day less glassy-eyed
than I.
            Last day human singular.
The outpouring of waters –
verification of gush
not trickle –

but the drought is tectonic:
plates of orange red rubble
on the rooftop garden
where only crows walk
above a shattered
rainbow of cars

ii.
In our new car
we debate the vaccine,
driving over puddles
that growl red from our paintwork.

I am somewhere in between
the first and second stages
of contractions; this is
a contained enormity

and all life, a vaccine
is a tinge, but, even then,
the virus itself hovers
like the leaf let go

still green with chlorophyll
not yet again the dirt

iii.
Before being returned to dirt
a woman I never forgot told me
a willy wagtail in the house
foretold a death,
she told me their name (djitti djitti)
the clicks they make
when they walk and twitch
towards song but do not sing,
a sound more like your heartbeat
than hooves or the iamb
with its soft breath.
If you are the bird
then I am the house
rafters all

iv.
After all, Rilke never had to make a life.
Grow one. He was visited
by the immaterial,
Angels, he called them,
and also moved inordinately
by statues, bloodless,
without even the flesh

of terra cotta.
What a thing it is
to have my blood swell like a king tide,
holding you against the shore of my ribs,
a murky clay form
not waiting for signature
or even its own scrawled name

v.
The chart has my scrawled name.
I have never been one for pain
I keep still and ignore
how it spreads: the twinges
down my legs, sharpening
at the side of my belly out.

Once I read of a poet still writing
though every word
was like casting a stone at himself
directly where others had already landed.

My only poetic secret
is ease, even though the branches
look twisted, they still, inexorably,
can be followed to light

vi.
I try to follow, light,
to thin and recede,
move away from
self-scrutiny, a face unseen.
'70s mirrors

at the end of poles,
a candle to illustrate

(Remember, she says, no one can make you do anything you
don't want to do)

And here are things
I have no desire to see,
the pupil dilated,
even now, the iris
a thin rim of colour
moving back

vii.
Moving back, I imagine my mother
herself bound down by my body;
my grandmother: six children,
outlived by five, outliving
her marriage (my grandfather lives on
happily in his third wife with three extra
children to show for it)

My husband, one of one,
parents of one marriage,
children of people
who died still loving
or at least tolerating
one another. My mother-in-law says
this is how it should be

viii.

But this is how it should be:
no skeletal family tree,
you moving through soil
laterally, running like a drain

that keeps the surface parallel
you meet another,
you intersect for a moment
you are stationary

then – you open, continue,

you don't know how many
have passed the green
before it threads

through you
and keeps moving

ix.
They keep me moving
but you do not budge,
asynclitic, your head in my hip
like a semi-colon tying two phrases
together. One inserts a hand,
twists, you turn back,
another tries, confirms your stubbornness.
Thirty hours and we are rolled

to another room. I refuse the mirror
held to see the cuts, refuse
even the gap in the covering sheets.
They say it will feel like a tug,
a prying loose and I am a window
frame being lightened of glass

x.
The beginning, a frame
still green with chlorophyll
holding up the rafters,
not waiting for a name,
following light
and moving back,
this is how it should be,
keep moving
lighter than the glass

form you will outlast,
the years flowing
from you like song,
hooves on soft sand
or numbered heartbeats

Four: It Is Hard to Become Accustomed to Being Food

Let Down

The ill-wired light switch
pulses in the wall.
Milk comes in with a throb
a burn. I no longer wonder
at you sleeping.

In all the earlier poems, I housed you
and now you scale
the outer edges of us both,
crying like a foghorn
captured in a bell.

I Write Poems When I Wake at 1.30am to Pump

I'm not sure there can be any good poems
about breast pumps
or involving the word colostrum.
I can tell you of my husband syringing
the yolk, yellow from my newly large nipples
or discovering that, if they bleed, the baby
will just spit the blood up
like the hatched djitti djitti regurgitates
the wiggling cicada from nest to table.
Outside the hospital window
the rock garden grown on the roof
glistened like a loaf covered in egg wash.
After you are born, I eat bread
copiously, scooping the soft
from the crust. There is nothing hard
about you. I once stepped, accidentally,
on a fallen fledgling
not even bones cracked
not even shell.

The breast not fed on for 36 hours

swells imperceptibly, is tight
like a gland you notice stretching
your neck and touching the tendons.
I've been biting the side of my tongue more
so the ridges resemble crumbling limestone.
I'm trying to just be sinew
the type from a horse used
to thread a lampshade together
in a tough winter, where even though
it's dark you smother the light.

A Fairytale

My breasts grow sore with overflow
stalling at the plug of cream
behind the duct, like cheesecake
baking. Left too long I grow
a fever, become an aquarium
for the fronds of bacteria floating
through, I haven't thought about
how large a colony must be
before it starts erecting hard cities
in the soft tissues of my breast.
Ten kilometres north, a girl dies to sepsis,
parents holding her after the hospital
hasn't helped in time. My poison
though is from life overtaking life.
I only started to kill the spiders webbing
our eaves once the babe was born,
only then was the threat of poison enough.
I grieved and looked away from the legs
too small to squash, they did not twitch
as eyelashes do, as the baby stutters out
of sleep and the bacteria in the milk
moves up and out
to greet his needy mouth.

In the part of the brain that regulates time

a bell sounds, it's been sounding most days
at 11, 12, 3, whenever you cough
and stir in your sleep and return to dreaming.
I am full as always with love and with
desire to be out of your reach. In my sleep
I orgasm. The after-effects of a virus
I hadn't anticipated. The dream is nothing
special. I am late for a plane, riding
a luggage cart over rumble strips, my
desire is inherently pedestrian. In the morning
I lie in bed and read a woman I knew once
interview her husband over lines of cocaine,
ketamine, there is sex even in how she describes
them talking. Later that day, I want to
devour every man I see, but I don't know
if it's just the flesh I'm after, the blood
in the steps. I would also lick the honey
butter off any woman's plump cheek. The book
I read reminds me of the mechanisms that
go into magic, that placing things side
by side only reveals the gaps. But also,
all the longing caught in the thick straw hair
tangled under a scarf. I feel this even as I lick my lips
to aggravate the cracks. There is no order
to beauty once the days and nights are
inseparable. I hold you, don't mistake
you for food, I feed you and don't
mistake the pleasure.

Withdrawal

When your milk dries up
you feel again the muscles
responsible for contracting
as the tooth feels the nerve retract
or rather, ceases to feel,
becomes, again, bone.

About the sacs pulsing
there is a pucker
of flesh, as if
it remembers the toothless
mouth still moist
from the womb.

If we ever imagined

it was not this slow awakening
but some sharp fresh thing
like dreaming, suddenly,
in another language

I never dream of cities
I haven't visited
even these imaginings are familiar
You slowly grow into our faces
a mirror that shifts
between solid and reflection

Somehow you frame us
come into the world
as you are
and intend to be

I read poems of others
alone on a bed
your voice still ringing
only inchoate to those
beyond you
as we all are

meeting slowly in the middle
of a tongue

one questions

if you know yourself
as wordless

and how long the gap is
before the word uncurls itself
and slithers to life

behind your newly sharp teeth

Winter

You will fear
when you are no longer held. Here
these are your own hands.

What begins (four weeks)

To draw a line
not in sand, ink, blood
but milk, or the veins
that run blue down the smooth slope
of my breast

There are no easy ways to deny you
I have tried tenderness
the tendresse of touch
an awe of skin

I try to be coral and cool
not rock and weed
I am trying to not be
the grit in your pearl

of a mouth, everything
you grow now
I haven't birthed
your pendulum swings

regardless

The Nothing

after Brook Emery

Is there a difference between
the texture of a lemon and an orange?
Sometimes I mispronounce words
to hear some hidden other syllable.
You are trying to talk now
you mouth full and puckering.
It is ritual these days to photograph
the months and when baby
can take a first bite of lemon,
the grimace, lips turned back
like a star descending into itself.
I don't know where we find the water
to irrigate all the fruit trees.
This is neither here nor there,
since you've been I've dreamt often
of the living reef, the kelp forests,
the weed that as it dangles to the surface
grows orbs one could only mistake
for lemons.

It's Cold Inside the Café

One of the mums
offers up a voluntary vaccine
meningococcal – old ghost
of warm waterholes,
holding a cool glass
to bruised skin to see the colour
fade. I miss deserts
and dessert, substitute
a strawberry world for
this cool saccharine.
The baby is sleeping well,
no side effects. Panadol
holding the fever at bay.
Britain committing to net zero
emissions. Panacea.
The difference
between voluntary and involuntary
vaccines is nine months,
the extended play
and the radio edit. Each of us
can pick our own baby's cry
from the colonnade of prams
lined up in a row
like the imported trees
we plant to hold
back the sun.

I No Longer Feel the Throb

First I noticed the pulse in my tongue
subsiding, how I could now
eat runny yolks again
        the matter spilt, heavier
        than when caked
        into a globe.

You start to recognise my voice.
You babble, late one night
and I realise you will never know
this language again – a tongue
between wake and sleep.

Your mind shimmers itself
out of dreams, you stick
your tongue out like a snake
at the end of speaking,
you are ready for the taste.

Your feet rise like teeth in the open

maw of the pram and like that you are awake

I dream I am inoculated against loss
a shot in the gum that holds things in place

Your face becomes a place I notice shadows
I have never loved like I am

in the process of losing – the water leak
that turns our mains off as it sinks

into sand while the foundations hold

Five: The Death Section

The Following Is True

The baby is not a cockroach
but does flail on the ground
limbs outstretched and cannot roll

which is a 'developmental milestone'
He is not a millstone, cannot clutch
enough to hang from my neck

We do not need to watch for stones
taken to the mouth and many years
until one may be thrown through a window

I will only know him on the brink
never decaying and he will know the world
once it moves past us –

how the time speeds towards the border
He will never share my dreams
of Florence, the pistachio green

waiting atop the Duomo to call my aunt
in the clear air filled with reception
to learn his great-grandmother has died

Florence is a place of bones
white and plaster, these
and starlings. The pure form of David

need not worry him
It will never be lost
only replicated

39.0

I place a hot water bottle
under the geriatric cat
to keep her warm
as she sleeps out seasons.
The double brick
holding extra-temperate winter
outside. These last few days
are chaos and loss,
the young poets who died
after summoning murmuration
never imagined so small
a faltering heartbeat
stilling so small a world.
They marshalled their handfuls of years
into flocks. I am stuck
on her back legs,
bringing the water
to her rough pink tongue,
opening the blinds
for a little sun.

Your son died

I think
he drowned. Years later
I would miss your funeral
and think of sending flowers
to your next husband
who had not ever lost a son
but had now lost you.
That was at the stage
when other people's tragedies
fell from me like scabs
though I healed slowly.
Moving, I found a manuscript
you had marked up,
some of the poems you loved
I'd forgotten I ever wrote.
In one my feet left cracks
on the ground wherever I stepped.
You died in the same month
as my father and so I grieved
but never sure if it was for you.
I wasn't graceful. You could
garden from other people's words
but you had a fury of a heart
even decades after loss. Even
now I'm unsure whom I'm mourning
as I write this, how to love
those that remain while pruning
all the flowers back
so the truth can grow.

Woo

I'm sure there's already a poem
about Nicolas Cage and John Travolta
and doves, how they had to cast Travolta
as the straight man, so when the souls swap
his smile gets cartoon-shark-wide, while Cage's
natural ebullience sombres somewhat. This is a life
lesson: if you have the kind of energy
that makes people think electricity
can travel in the air between bulbs
someone will always figure out
a way to wire you down. Somewhere
in my neighbourhood a dog is barking.
Parenthood makes you bloodthirsty.
I would choke it silent for another
five minutes of sleep. Travolta grieves
the accidental sniper shot of his son,
now what types of thirst would that engender?
Would that I never know and never come to
a church on fire to emerge through
the smoke of grief a changed man
to a chorale of bullets that somehow
always miss the doves flying into rafters.

The End Results of Need

I am meant
to be writing
about the loss
of the world

the throttle
that alternates
in the throats

of songbirds
between speech
and the backward
wings

of retreat

Poem to My Aunt

I write this from verdancy:
summer flies in the late April garden
my belly swelling outward
like the frog's song-bound throat

Common to all this: sound
and colour, though none of the purples
that soothed you are visible
only the everyday green

some flecks of red banksia
the arms of the neighbour's trees stretched
over our fence. If I was
to say more of us die alone

that would be a lie, even to say
none of us are alone
stretches theology or microbiology
into my garden of solid things

But it is not a lie to say you weren't abandoned
that your hand was held and balm applied
to your lips by those who loved you
I do not grieve, but am green

with loss, growing up and out – ripe
with all the not alone-ness
I can feel kicking at my centre
and buzzing at my head, my arms

circling like a conductor's for the way
into the song that will hold you

and say your name when you are dust
or prayer returned to air

2020

I remember the hot iron
language becomes after loss

not just names, but the names
of things become resentful:

how does a chair cohere
when they do not – death

is ludicrous, leads to filleting
the useless spoons from the third drawer down

to becoming ruthless in garages
a war of screws, attrition

of appliances, while in the vena cava
of the home's walls

something of their scent
still circulates

I Am Made Fuzzy by Grief

We all tread lightly
around dead parents

Imagine the one left
as the living bird

waiting for its mate
by the feather-scattered tarmac

If I was to say 'on' the road
it would be too tragic

My own mate cannot visualise
I say knife and he spells it out

I say knife of loss
and I think he hears it

mourning in his silent way
without ghosts

Covered in Crumbs and Contagion

My cat can no longer crouch
but hovers, belly just above floor.

She is 18, kidneys going,
front legs strong, her back

emaciated like the empty half
of a puppet. It is the year

we are all only at home,
I watch her try and make a bed

on the hard ground, stretching out
into weeks, my stomach buzzing

imperceptibly with life. I have loved
and watched the loved become dust.

Before bed each night my husband
puts a water bottle below puss

settles her into a soft cocoon
of red velvet; I too wish

to be any type of permanent home.

A House Big Enough to Never Leave

The end result is always the same –
the roof gives, rafters poke through plaster
like greenstick fractures, a family photo
hangs askew; one from a driving tour
of Europe is cracked on the ground.
They say grief eventually leaves
the body like nail clippings flushed
but a house is different, entirely
solid, even in disaster the rubble breaks a toe,
you're picking glass out of your hair.
You say that's the frame of his chair over there.
Is this the darkness that wails in caves
for us to find tongues for shadows,
to pluck stalactites from the ceilings
and suckle them, our breasts black and blue
like some mirror of a far-off sky.

First Holiday

My baby loves his dinosaur.
He won't let go of it in the car.

He catches its tail in his mouth
pokes its eyes with his fingers

as we drive slowly the one-way road
up the mountain. Parenting is a language

of firsts until it becomes a language
of lasts. My son strapped

to his father cackles the whole way
we walk, the trees giving nothing

to the sky, a still day
disturbed not even by needle

drifting. We joke, say he thinks he controls
all this. But he cannot know

himself as separate enough to exert power
over anything, even his own legs

do not hold under him yet. Though
I imagine him holding us years from now

our bodies sloughing off skin, how
he must tenderly and without caution

love us.

Love

You have ten fingers,
ten toes, a cry I can pick
from the wind over a building site.
You have eyes greedy
with life, when I try to feed you,
you grab the spoon, the sickness
in all babies is being a baby.
Seconds after being built,
closer to falling apart.
You make me doubt every way
I loved, you make my feet
vibrate with tiredness,
I'm on an overpass
with trucks thundering under
or on stone cliffs with waves
that mean nothing and dissolve
wholly into sound
only to come again, relentless
there is no end, only the edges
of loss that mark each calendar day
with a bright smile, firsts,
as you wobble slightly closer
to the edge of my life.

Six: #2020

Self-plagiarism: Ode to WillyWeather

All the ways I've been taught
to look for trends are oceans.
Offshore now beyond the one crest
breaking across sand and reef
more boats come to moor
as we debate how many we'll let mourn.

My husband is the only head
left out back the far break
closest to the groyne, where
on a normal day men would sit
clutched together like birdshit
under a berry tree.

Everyone I know is loving
each other more, at least
in these first weeks of plague

while surfers like bats or sharks
creep in beyond the flags.

Escape

You wake at 12, 4, 6, and 8.
Maybe I should give up.
The flies are out, the flowers dying.
Other poets write of war
but we are all coughing into our elbows.
Such is the year of your birth.
I say, I wouldn't be seen dead
and it's true I've never viewed an open casket.
My friends keep their mother home
till she's too stiff to move.
We put ours in the cheapest box
we can find that looks real.
These are the decisions
you'll one day make for me
unless I find a way
to cradle you, till it's you
rising from the shroud.

You have to

swirl breast milk
to reconstitute it

like mixing together anything old
removed from the cupboard.

We still manage to get brunch
several days a week

to eat eggs
that are not my own.

It's gruelling
to be such a basic thing

as food. Do you
know that babies

died from being given
cow's milk only

and too early?
So many things

die now. I did not
you do not

there's a graph
that looks like starlings

in flight scattering.
It shows by size

all the words
we've tried to use

to say we're sorry to the world
'devastated, shit, corruption'

Not Imagining Elsewhere

It was the year the world closed
itself into some dream of bodies

There was sovereignty then
no risk of disclosure or exposure

The baby slept poorly
We were alone rarely

but a triumvirate often
Others still went out

caught themselves at parties
talking about luck

The sky looks like a crumpled car door
if you wake too early

You huffed and snorted
like the owl in a lullaby

wouldn't sleep long enough
for me to finish the poem

or the year

Of Human Bondage

The water still drips off the plants from
where I showered them
& the haze drops
temperatures by 7 degrees

The book I'm reading
was printed in the last great year
of the flu
its author surviving
& continuing

only to write about art – I think
he is the one with a famous son
also an author

For you my son I only wish currently
art
though

of course
underneath it

survival

I love the way that Ammons

uses the colon like a carbon molecule:
holding an other; nothing is ever
not sentimental, especially punctuation
you can make a home in
by drawing a line – straight
between two points.

Can you untrain the ways
we have of joining?

The summer my baby is born
seven people die from sharks
and I try to keep him thriving.
We worry about catching fevers
fretting our world
is no longer temperate. I clutch

and allow myself to be clutched
loved and loved.

Bathers Beach

Even the end is picturesque

the people spaced evenly

like pylons along the pier.

Not moving they inspect the catch

thinned as Giacometti's statues.

We are told we are at war

but even this is invisible.

Everywhere families bring children

on scooters and the rest of us

travel two-by-two

like the survivors from the ark –

those not let leave.

Cruel

The sour of the night's sleep
tingles my tongue
like showbag sherbet
found in the bottom of a cupboard

The sky has clouded over
preparing not to rain
but to linger sulking
like a shaved cat

What I'm not telling you
is my baby is sick
lying on the ground
'not our lil guy,' day care says

We haven't gone to pick him up
are waiting for some greater sign
of illness. Cruelty
to withhold something so simple

You can be cruel without notice
You can be cruel just balancing
coffee cup and conversation
ignoring a need.

The truth about the end of the world

is that you can stay in your bed
as you always do, and read
about it by the light of electrons
held in the right state
of buzz. You can
throw away friendships by that light.
Say you haven't heard for days
about the sunrise on their side
of the green bed of planet
or you've forgotten all the bits
about them that weren't ragged
like sore gums being brushed
after a long night. You will
probably forget even the beautiful
words for gums and jaws: gingivae, mandible,
maxilla; like drawing a tree back
from verdancy to stick figure.
You will be alone in a bathroom
wondering about the damned light,
if it's the same as the sacred
and if even the sacrificed get that moment
of illumination before they pan
back to the toothpaste
dried to the mirror.

Day Care Day

Every day
my son
is away
he cries
without ceasing
stopping only
to sleep
he will
not eat
not drink
he desiccates
the worm
of love
turns sour
his pain
is indecent
renders us
indecorous red
with loss
his face
folds in
only teeth
and tears
we want
love to
be loved
but not
the wrenching

limbs free
the unceremonial
drop on
the floor

Every Day I Call the Honeyeater by the Wrong Name

Wattlebird on the steps without wattle
        without the soft wobbling fold of skin
        that wrinkles as it calls
high and rough like something sharp
        falling on tin and scraping down
to where the banksias also lay
        detritus underfoot
hard and cutting, like being forgotten
by a friend turned stranger on the street
        where you both once grew wild
and weedy, the ends of bleach-blond hair
        falling to the stone like pollen
as your fingers caught the bark and tore
        your way up the limbs
to the crook where the bird
        dove with its prehistoric knowledge
of threat and that keening cry
        that cannot distinguish this
from any other egg-stealing epoch
        and this I also cannot name
have forgotten, what to call
        the time when we lived together
        before that, too, ended.

I want to write a joyful poem

          to startle the year
into a state of joy
to shock the old year
to shock the shackles
          of the old year
it's been tight
it's been a tight old year
we counted biscuits, beans,
broken bones, we beaded
          the days into rosaries
and the prayer was this:
          'joy, oh joy
let me be overtaken
let this old blood hum
let the world be overtaken
          so it can be respun'

Seven: These Poems Are Mostly Private Letters, Poems after Randolph Stow

Calliope

i.

'Silence longs for nothing'
Randolph Stow 'Setthathirath'

I grew the mulberry bush on the mount.
Waited for the worms to come, spin.

My milk came in. You drank easy.
Lazy, hours, then days passed.

Your tongue became spirited.
You sputtered, spat, didn't speak.

Sang, then never drank again.
To you, I would say, silence

does have its own longing.
Not for speech but for an echo.

The threads quiver in the wind,
they cannot be plucked or fired

but are full of arrows nonetheless.
You should know the world has no need

of voices, but wants, like the wind
winding through leaves.

ii.
Some say Orpheus died to the trees
that whoever tore him limb from limb
grew rocks and stuck monster to the green
ground. Ovid knew how to change for longing

but his forests moved swiftly
like the pines that track the cooler weather uphill
while the other branches falter. Lovely
you are nine months of longing, still

this is too fast to know if you are roots
or dismemberment, if you too will give
to the glacier that grinds the rocks to rubble
or the water that rises after.

iii.
What hauntings come out of earth
are rooted, carry forth dirt. Don't
sing love, don't sing. Your longing
has already lost you a wife, a lyre
to the heavens. Does your tongue lie
when it tastes or only in song
does it betray salt into sweetness?

It matters what you sing now, the earth
quakes of it. This is not yours but you
are mine. I mourn you in all the winds;
I cannot conceal the heaviness
of laying each of your limbs
into a separate grave of song.

Dear Son / A Wind From the Sea

There's no dust
but your throat is so dry

with air
you wake anyway

I can't name
the ways you come

to sleep or don't
but time makes

the morning tick over
I apologise

for liking you silent
the brick walls of our house

sprayed down
and steaming in the heat

The other side of the country
under cloud, figureless,

I brush you from my hands

Child Portraits with Background

The suburbs are soft
and paper dry as neonate skin,
sky the blue tissue of wedding boxes.

Into this a child is born
finds his way through some
iron-clad luck, living

so every day is easy,
astute, polished as shell
separated from flesh

a middle ground towards sand,
air. This child is born
to neither forest nor downs

and to only two seasons
air-conditioning and sunburn.

Landscapes

Your voice builds like the butcher
calling out orders in mid-afternoon
after-school peak in the Melville Coles.

In the afternoon you are most in love
with walls, the welling colour of the aisles.

Mornings, you are never not there. Our days unroll
over the change to autumn, stroller rolling lit-up
by the convection fridges.

Outside, is it raining? Do the crows gather in the car park?
Their eyes glinting like ground covered in wet desert quartz.

Sea Children, See Children

My eyes flit, do not settle
it used to be I'd tell poets
poetry is learning to see

I don't even wake with words
in my mouth now, nor teeth
I only want good things for the world

but I'm too lazy to list
all the extinct species that prevent this

Let it be known
the days are all death
and I cannot write of stingrays except
to acknowledge the barb

I disappoint myself, releasing
the catch back, guiding
your hands to trace my face

You will never know more than you know
the world contracts around the word

I close my eyes so you can feel
where the bone gives to socket
like banks to harbour

Eight: Even Unfit Mothers Have Fit Arms

Uniform

after Tracy Ryan

i.
My own cut
came 30 hours
into the process
my hands raw
from rinsing
the fabric

everything was then
sterilised, I was
shaved back
curtains drawn
o'head lights
on

my baby never
got the chance to choose
or rather, the choice
he made was stubbornness

keeping his head
to the one angle
not to unbend
nothing left
to stitch

ii.
Motherhood is bloodless.
I am ashamed to say.
This far into the suburbs,
the danger is not
to smell the shit.
I am always taking to my bed
and forgetting to take my glasses off,
the rest of the day
I am blind.
This is an island
within an island,
a rocky crag
circled by a blue hole.
I don't: write
my thank you notes,
my shopping lists,
my change of address.
I am barely
writing this poem.

iii.
Tracy, you did this twice
and wrote it more.
Twice the number of hands
grabbing you in
weakness and in love
(what is love
    but weakness).
You lived in homes
you called skeletons
but you yourself were no
skeleton. You can
talk the romance

language we all know
is guttural phlegm
and the end of civilisations
in fire. In my home
we wrap extra padding
about the cushions
avoiding anything hard.

My Whole Life

The father blows on the toast, steaming in the autumn air
so his daughter's mouth doesn't burn, beside them
a big lab turns circles for trees.
I can see the planning that has gone into this situation
the job, the slightly shitty rentals, proposal in Europe
first house bought (a duplex) small yard, hence
the dog. The baby comes into the world in autumn,
they don't know how to dress it, they wait a week
to bathe it, the dog goes unwalked, her nipples split
and the babe vomits pink. But somehow
they keep going, walking the block every two hours
for a nap, dog at home, seasons change in their new
unpredictable ways. The rain comes, goes again
for weeks, then floods, after there are fires
you can only tell by the smoke, and then they find themselves
again in autumn. The child can walk, say 'dog'
'bark' and eats things other than its mother.
My whole life I was blind to this.

I Do Not Feel Beheaded

Medusa kept her head
of heads a lot longer
than her headlessness,
being that once stone
she was insensate,
incensed, as her screaming mouths
should tell you, but an object
like a basketball, not headless
like the chicken that perambulates
while gushing red.
                                        This other poet
(I know another, again) describes
my body as orb, singular,
no cranium. But my body –
round yes – is a head
spinning limbs off it
like the open mouths of snakes
hissing; I say: I need not be tender
to be a life-bringer
and an ender.

Your Taste in People Will Change When You Learn to Love Yourself

The only time I am repulsed
by my baby is when he cries
to touch cold water and cries
at the sound of waves. Listen, I think
this is the sound you and I made together
in my snow globe belly, you a penguin
in summertime in plastic snow
still beautiful. I don't want to breastfeed
anymore but I do it, my cobra
eating another's eggs, you are open-mouthed
and throat bobbing. In every way
I make myself ugly. Yes, I know
this is all love, but I would rather
salt flesh for sea voyages
than wounds.

Don't All Mothers Wish Immortality

Newborns they can suckle the life out of you and you can let them, lying back in the tan rocker you picked to match the wood accents of your artful dune green nursery. You can almost feel how they split your life and those years are loose and once you can remember writing a poem about the muses your mother and father and love you can't remember in the kitchen and can you ever know if this is how it started that cancan of recriminations, husked loves and split weekends? You can know Medea didn't kill her brother or her children but sent them to immortality and you are imagining Hera's altar stone stuffed with goose down because once you too were a woman who turned down gods and sewed their feathered wings into cushions with even stabbing stitches and you can feel the babe pulling milk through like threads and you can believe you are indeed knitting him together and you can forgive both him and yourself this.

The Sermon on the Mount

Mary, namesake,
beloved, you got
fucked over
to face the barn
the straw, unhygienic
donkeys baying
at dawn.
And for what?
You never got
the good crude
half of being
screwed. Famous
mothers throughout history,
I implore you:
stop loving
what will only
bleed you out.

Brothers, Leeches and Being Turnt Inside Out

after Tracy Ryan

i.
I fear having given birth to myself
or my brother. He is the pale type,

disappointed he doesn't faint
at the sight of his own blood

I would put a dog in a ring
another to go for the throat

I often lie about this. Wear
bracelets of cotton, call them leathers

I have always enjoyed silence
a heartbeat is loud – insistent

You cry like an iamb and this
is the betrayal of poetry

no heart, but an anger of breath

ii.
Back to the leeches. When I heard
my brother was to be born

I ran into the bush, ignored
the cry that followed, vicious

in disappointment. Sometimes
loving another person can be a lie

The leech injects a toxin in
to stop the blood coagulating

a family wound will do this
A poem need not be a puzzle

Everything I've written here is true
I do love you

iii.
Being turnt
is another way of saying
v. v. v. drunk

Because of my baby
I cannot get
v. v. v. drunk

iv.
Being turned inside out
as the leech is, in your poem
does not render
the unfamiliar, familiar,
just bloody

v.
After seven months
and the nine of growing you

my insides remember
how to turn themselves
from the inside to
fall into the toilet
like leeches
letting go

vi.
There's an older woman
at my coffee store
every day for
babycinos
her granddaughter
is often dirty
I cannot see you
as other than
naked
after a shower
that I made you
clean

In Writing About Cain

'Dreams are the suicides of the well-behaved'
Fay Zwicky

In writing about Cain
I forget about Martha
guilty of the same thing,
her bloody sister Mary
sitting by the unswept fireplace
angling her head up
and not quite touching His feet

Martha in the kitchen preparing the meal
Martha at the table, Martha
with the broom again and the crumbs
still spilling out as she goes to put
another log on so all is kept warm
knowing it'll mean a juggle later
to chop the wood and dice
the vegetables and nobody
ever thinks about how

Martha doesn't kill Mary
because she's too busy
to even be like Cain
with his fanciful sacrifice
and time to gloat

Sometimes if I read a very good poem

I will say, 'She knows what's up.'
They are nearly always poems written
about Orpheus and always (she)
poems by women. Orpheus is the worst
if you are a woman, with all his
lute playing and passion.
There is nothing practical about
an addiction to memory,
he is always living in the past
is something my mother says
about her first husband –
my father. I always thought
I'd have a daughter raised
for the muse not birth from muse
to mother.

Don't Doubt

Would you like:
    a subtle reminder
    of your mortality?

Try:
    wedlock
    children in coffee shops
    pulling the marshmallow eyes
    off babycinos

I only like:
    coffee
    warm enough to burn

Having a baby is nothing like:
    a watermelon
you aren't allowed to cut it open
for starters

It is everything like:
    continuously scrolling
        sold items on various online
            market places
                at 4am

I can still be myself even if:
    I love you

I can still be myself
if loving you involves

always purchasing ways out
of loving you

and then waking you in the night
just to hear you breathe

I eat my grapefruit

scooping out the chambers
of the heart with a spoon.

It is impossible to discuss
the grapefruit without also
the flesh, the grapefruit

lacks sentiment but has veins
of the vibrant pink
swirling against

the off-white
of the hollow.
I am huddled over

ignoring the buzz
and swell of shadows
and insects, picking

out the last grains
of juice, and popping them
against my tongue.

No one is ever
appropriately ugly
with need. I want

to ask where
is your own language
of desire? I picture

the raw *en pointe* toes
of dancers in movies
in their grapefruit pink shoes

this, I say,
is how you move
the poem.

Six Months

Perhaps I have too easily given up
faith right when the world seems
equal parts awe-full and awful.

I feel the circumference of another planet
circle within me, with the clarity of day and night
I have too easily given up.

At the time of my father's death, I knew
I would never say his name again
without breathing equally awe-full and awful.

Now I look for stars to spell of you both –
a braille of light against my back.
Perhaps I have too easily given up

and you will suckle against the last of the light
while the skin of the world crawls
all parts awful and awful

and you will only speak your own tongue
and hold your own name and I will love
and love anyway, easily given up
for the awe of you, even awful.

Nine: From Tumbleweed to Tick

i.
Currently you are
rolling inside me, a tumbleweed
looking for a ditch to stick,

tangle of metaphors, I have lost
the thread   the edges
are burning.   What I can offer you
is the inland of a salt lake
where I try to keep the smoke
from circulating.

ii.
On our coast
nobody burns
although the northerly
would change that if
it could. You are
soundless unlike
the aluminium foil crackle
of the roof lifting,
You are the points of the pine
that immolate first,
one of the soft pains
lost in my body.

iii.
Another new year

another jetty
despite the doctor's incitation
not to leap
and the very measured ways
we note the rest of our days.
He has forgotten
the food
but is eager
to feed me:
calcium, dried fruit and nuts.

I am eager
to just be bones
and a growing thing
stretched taut;
the tomato
before it bursts
the skin
and turns.

iv.
I stop eating for comfort
and start eating for grief
trying to find the thing
that stops a real pain
at the top of my gut.

A student coins the term:
globular banality;
which summarises
very well
how I feel at all
my expansions.

v.
Already I feel
as set and round
as a well-screwed
lightbulb unable
to fall or bounce
without shattering.

This then is the tedium
of the glass in which
the filament glows
with certain magic –
a diagram you can draw
from age 12 onwards,
a gap, a switch,
a joining.

vi.
Do we begin to share the same heart?

You will only die once,
though I may have many deaths
live and then pass inside me.
The earth moves us to consider
compost, decay; what can be so
and what floats out to sea.

vii.
I've heard limitation is freeing.
I teach it even, that by placing
things in order, some other
part of you opens; to contain
your sleep you order my ribs

outwards like counting sticks
before setting them afloat
on a river on fire.

viii.
We wake early
in preparation:

the morning is cooler then.

When I was twelve,
in the Northern Territory
I learnt the rules of shade,
the baby screaming
from the earliest light.

The only time I ever
pretended an interest in mothering
was that summer, which is
also the only time
I got to tell the other children
to stay off the roads at dusk
because of dingos

and not to put our heads under
still, warm water. Things breed
too much in the heat
and then starve. The morning
was the only time

it was nice to touch skin to skin
the baby, still febrile
cooling in my arms.

ix.
I think of you, green fuse,
little flame, contained fire

and aftermath, the veins on my body
emerging like dried riverbeds

your father watching footage on his phone
of the happenings over east,

a cumulus of smoke moving across roads
then ignition, and the house is gone.

x.
The cirrus turns the ocean to glare
bright silver of an afternoon.
In every spell, fire is necessary,
the potion is molten, even metal
is made liquid and then transformed.
Your father is out, running along the beach
his feet catching and tossing the smallest
remnants of stars made rock and broken
again by water, earth turning with the oceans
at a subtly different rate to the air
spinning like a layer cake overhead.

I am resting because you are not resting
but multiplying, my blood sung up
25% so I burn on still and stormy days at 38 degrees
and yet I do not catch fire and keep to solid
lines, although at times I blur, in the ocean I am
small when I am also your ocean

like the different levels of atmosphere
blowing different directions but always

close.

xi.
One night in the 30-degree midnight easterly
of flies and even peewees venturing inside
and pecking for water, a smoke comes up
and your father climbs by moonlight
to stand by the rusted bore tanks and look
across all horizons for the red shimmer
of Mars or flame. Even though it's dark, it's hot enough
the grasses could pass from blade to blade
a fire. We say we will wait by water if it comes.
The ocean 50 metres away and horribly still
like a mirror waiting to become the face that tells
your future. And yes, we have been beautiful
for so long.

xii.
All the ways we drive out of Perth
are through fire, Leach Highway
to Tonkin to Great Eastern.
It's not our fire, baby, but the east's
come to us on the radio, the spectre
of satellites showing a grey cloud
moving across half the world to reach us.

The line of the hills slackens
like my pelvic bone
made awkward by relaxin,

told not to push too hard
or my hips might flex and give to a pain
I won't feel yet. But you are for a short time
blood for blood like smoke on the wind,
not yet the ocean currents that insistently
separate land from land or drift
us closer.

xiii.
A flood puts out the fires
as I bake you in the fuel
that keeps my mind in fever.

xiv.
You are the most singular of singulars
everything about you writ large.
At thirteen weeks your brain
like a planet comes into focus.

xv.
A boy.
I always imagined
a daughter.

Flame among flames
your red blood that
mimics my red blood,
my heart beats
like the barks
of Weddell seals
on the melting ice

yours with the whir
of a machine starting
and this = a clue
you are not to be
like me after all

and there it is
you are more the roar
of circuitry than the blood
I pump around you, foreign
as the bird
diving for the tick

and would it not be the same
unsameness if you were mine daughter
XX not XY?
Your flame still
the gaps in the song.

Acknowledgements and works cited

These poems were written, and the poet lives, on unceded Whadjuk Noongar boodjar.

My husband Colin did the work of being with our son so that I could do the work of writing these poems. Thanks to those who fed us: Rose, Mija and Christine especially. Our wider family and friend networks provided nourishment in other ways. Curtin University gave me employment, supportive colleagues and inspiring students. Thanks to my other work friends – 'Melville babies 2020' – for the daily WhatsApps, playgroups and coffee dates. Thanks, as always, to the team at Fremantle Press for taking on this manuscript and running with it, and for her judicious editorial eye and inspiration, especial thanks to Tracy Ryan. Thanks also to Omar Sakr for looking at an early version of the manuscript and declaring it to, in fact, be a book. Funding was provided by the Australia Council and the Department of Local Government, Sport and Cultural Industries (WA).

'Crowning' was previously published in *Best of Australian Poems 2022.*
'I Write Poems When I Wake at 1.30am to Pump' was previously published in *Meanjin*.
'In Process' was previously published as 'In Process: Seven Months (almost)' in *Westerly*.
'The Nothing' responds to pp. 31–33 of Brook Emery's *Collusion*.
'A House Big Enough to Never Leave' was previously published in *Portside Review*.
'Uniform', title taken from Tracy Ryan's 'Uniform', *Bluebeard in Drag*, p. 17, with permission from Fremantle Press.
'In Writing About Cain', epigraph from Fay Zwicky, 'Passing', Collected Poems of Fay Zwicky, p. 148, reproduced with permission from UWA Press.

'Brothers, Leeches, and Being Turnt Inside Out', after Tracy Ryan's 'Leeches', *Bluebeard in Drag*, p. 54, with permission from Fremantle Press.

'These Poems Are Mostly Private Letters', section title taken, with permission from Fremantle Press, from Randolph Stow's introduction to his work in Alexander Craig's *Twelve Poets, 1950–1970*, published by Jacaranda Press and quoted in John Kinsella's introduction to *The Land's Meaning*, p. 42.

'Calliope', 'Landscapes', and 'See Children, Sea Children' were previously presented as part of the 2021 Randolph Stow Memorial Lecture and published in *Westerly*.

'Calliope', epigraph from Randolph Stow's 'Setthathirath', *The Land's Meaning*, p. 169, with permission from Fremantle Press.

"Child Portraits with Background', title and allusions from Randolph Stow's 'Child Portraits, with Background', *The Land's Meaning*, p. 74, with permission from Fremantle Press.

'Landscapes', title taken from Randolph Stow's 'Landscapes', *The Land's Meaning*, p. 113, with permission from Fremantle Press.

'Sea Children, See Children', title taken from Randolph Stow's 'Sea Children' (*The Land's Meaning*, p. 71). The line 'you will never know more than you know' is a rephrasing of Stow's 'Country Children know more than they know', from his poem 'Country Children' (*The Land's Meaning*, p. 72), and the concluding line 'like banks to harbour' is a rephrasing of 'beyond the arm of the harbour, on the banks', from 'Sea Children', with permission from Fremantle Press.

Works Cited:

Emery, Brook. *Collusion*. John Leonard Press, 2012.

Ryan, Tracy. *Bluebeard in Drag*. Fremantle Arts Centre Press, 1996.

Stow, Randolph. *The Land's Meaning. New Selected Poems*. Fremantle Press, 2012.

Zwicky, Fay. *The Collected Poems of Fay Zwicky*. UWAP, 2017.

First published 2023 by
FREMANTLE PRESS

Fremantle Press Inc. trading as Fremantle Press
PO Box 158, North Fremantle, Western Australia, 6159
fremantlepress.com.au

Cover design Anna Maley-Fadgyas, booksdesigns.com.au
Cover images: *Cortinarius rotundisporus*, Denmark, 2004, Katrina Syme; *Eucalyptus conferruminata, Bald Island Marlock*, 2002, Philippa Nikulinsky AM.
Printed and bound in Australia by Griffin Press.

A catalogue record for this book is available from the National Library of Australia

ISBN 9781760992590 (paperback)
ISBN 9781760992606 (ebook)

Fremantle Press is supported by the State Government through the Department of Local Government, Sport and Cultural Industries.

Fremantle Press respectfully acknowledges the Wadjak people of the Noongar nation as the Traditional Owners and Custodians of the land where we work in Walyalap.